AMERICAN INDIAN LIFE

The Navajo
The Past and Present of the Diné

by Donna Janell Bowman

Consultant:
Brett Barker, PhD
Associate Professor of History
University of Wisconsin–Marathon County

CAPSTONE PRESS
a capstone imprint

Fact Finders Books are published by Capstone Press,
1710 Roe Crest Drive, North Mankato, Minnesota 56003
www.capstonepub.com

Library of Congress Cataloging-in-Publication Data
Bowman, Donna Janell.
The Navajo: the past and present of the Diné / by Donna Janell Bowman.
pages cm.—(Fact finders. American Indian life)
Includes bibliographical references and index.
Audience: Grades 4-6.
Summary: "Explains Navajo history and highlights Navajo life in modern
society"—Provided by publisher.
ISBN 978-1-4914-4992-9 (library binding)
ISBN 978-1-4914-5004-8 (paperback)
ISBN 978-1-4914-5008-6 (ebook pdf)
1. Navajo Indians—History—Juvenile literature. 2. Navajo Indians—Social
life and customs—Juvenile literature. I. Title.
E99.N3S58 2016
 979.1004'9726—dc23   2015009634

Editorial Credits
Catherine Neitge, editor; Tracy Davies McCabe, designer;
Svetlana Zhurkin, media researcher; Kathy McColley, production specialist

Photo Credits
Alamy: Chuck Place, 5 (top), Goddard New Era, 18, North Wind
Picture Archives, cover (bottom left), WorldFoto, 26; AP Photo: *The
Salt Lake Tribune*/Rick Egan, 21; Arthur Shilstone, 15; Getty Images:
Panoramic Images, 27 (left), Paul Chesley, 5 (bottom), Robert Alexander,
6; iStockphoto: nicoolay, cover (top), 1, stevenallan, 24 (left); Library of
Congress, 10, 24 (right); Newscom: Rex/Patrick Frilet, 23; North Wind
Picture Archives: Nancy Carter, 16, 25 (bottom), NativeStock, 11, 13, 20,
22, 27 (right); Shutterstock: Chris Geszvain, cover (bottom right), coral, 28,
digitalfarmer, 25 (top), jejim, 12, JeniFoto, 29, Tom Grundy, 7, Tom Tietz, 9,
Tomaz Kunst, 8; U.S. Marine Corps, 19; XNR Productions, 17

Printed in Canada.
032015   008825FRF15

Table of Contents

The Healing Way

A medicine man kneels on the dirt floor of a hogan. He is there to treat a young girl with a fever. Her family and friends participate in the traditional Healing Way ceremony too. Carefully the man dips his hand into colorful sands. Pictures and symbols emerge as he shifts the sand between his fingertips.

When the picture is finished, the young patient sits in the center of it. It is believed the sand will absorb negative energy. All the while, the medicine man sings, prays, and chants. He is calling to the spirits to heal the girl.

When it is over, the young patient leaves. She might be feeling better. She might see a medical doctor. The beautiful sand painting is destroyed.

Being Navajo means maintaining cultural **traditions** in a modern world.

tradition: custom, idea, or belief passed down through time

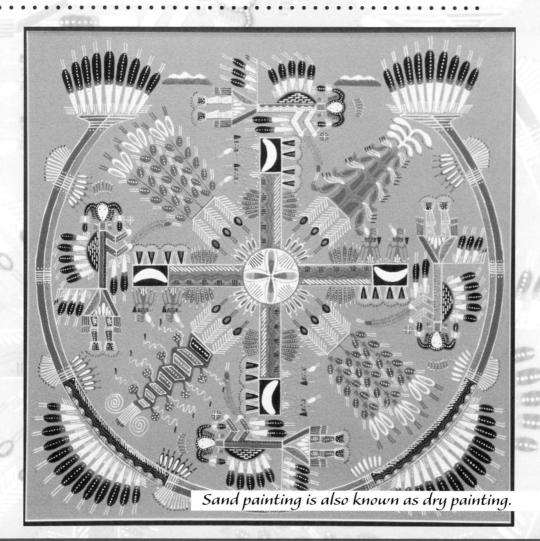

Sand painting is also known as dry painting.

Sand painting

There are two kinds of Navajo sand paintings. One is made by a medicine man, known as a singer. The sand paintings are important parts of traditional healing and blessing ceremonies. They are made and destroyed in a day. They are rarely viewed by non-Navajos. There are also sand paintings made as permanent works of art.

Chapter 1

People of the Land

The Dineh Tah Navajo Dancers promote cultural understanding through dance.

Ancestors of today's Navajo were hunter-gatherers. They migrated from present-day Alaska and Canada about 500 to 1,000 years ago. They settled in the canyons of northwestern New Mexico. They called themselves the Diné (pronounced deh-NEH). It means the people. Their new homeland was Dinétah. It means among the people. They believed they were caretakers of the land. Four sacred mountains mark the boundaries of their traditional homeland—Arizona's San Francisco Peaks, Colorado's Hesperus Mountain and Blanca Peak, and New Mexico's Mount Taylor.

Four sacred mountains

The Navajo's sacred mountains are linked to colors and directions. Hesperus Mountain to the north represents black. Blanca Peak to the east is linked to white. Mount Taylor to the south is linked to turquoise. San Francisco Peaks (above) to the west represent yellow.

ancestor: family member who lived a long time ago

HOMES AND FARMING

Navajo homes were made from logs covered with mud. They were called hogans. Some hogans were round while others had six or eight sides. A hogan's door always faced east toward the morning sun. The roof represented the sky and the floor represented Earth.

In the summer Navajo moved to a hogan that was open on one side. Before moving into a new hogan, a medicine man blessed it. During a hogan ceremony, people sat in a pattern. Men sat against the south wall. Women sat against the north wall. Children sat near their mother. And **elders** had a place of honor against the west wall.

Hogans today are used in ceremonies.

The Navajo Nation's beautiful Monument Valley stretches into Arizona and Utah .

The Navajo lived in scattered family groups called **clans**. People were born into their mother's clan. After marriage, a husband became part of his wife's clan. Navajo women owned the hogans, land, and livestock, passing them down to their daughters. Having ownership gave women some power.

elder: older person whose experience makes him or her a leader
clan: a large group of families and related people

DESERT LIFE

Like the neighboring Pueblo Indians, including the Hopi, the Navajo adopted an agricultural lifestyle. They also hunted wild game with bows and arrows. To adapt to desert farming, they created underground irrigation systems. Corn became especially important. The Navajo used pollen from corn tassels in blessings and ceremonies. In many American Indian cultures, corn, beans, and squash are called the three sisters. They are planted together. Each of the plants benefits the others.

Unlike many American Indian tribes, the Navajo weren't led by traditional chiefs. There was no single authority over all the people. Instead, each family clan chose a leader. Because the clans lived apart from other clans, members of each group governed themselves.

Famed photographer Edward S. Curtis pictured corn growing between canyon walls in the early 1900s.

NAVAJO CLOTHING

To the Navajo long hair symbolizes life and memory. It is part of their identity, much like their clothes. In the distant past Navajo clothing was simple. It was made from deerskin or woven yucca fibers. Turquoise from the area was made into beads and jewelry. They believed the blue-green stone had protective powers from Mother Earth. To protect their feet and legs, they made leather or woven moccasins. During winter months, deerskin ponchos or rabbit-fur cloaks kept them warm. They later began wearing clothing introduced by the Spanish. Navajo women began wearing wool and cloth skirts and blouses.

Apache relatives

Navajo people are relatives of the Apache. They split into two groups when they migrated from Alaska and Canada. Early Spanish explorers called them *apaches du nabaju* (Apaches of the cultivated fields), which was shortened to Navajo.

Traditional clothes included wool dresses, moccasins, and leggings.

Chapter 2

Suffering and Fear

Unlike the Navajo and other American Indians, European explorers believed land was to be conquered and owned by individuals. Spain had claimed the Southwest in 1493, but explorers didn't arrive for more than 50 years. They were looking for gold but didn't find any. Then, in 1598, a Spaniard named Juan de Oñate brought settlers to the lands of the Navajo and Pueblo. Spanish settlers brought herds of cattle, sheep, goats, and pigs. Missionaries set out to convert Indians to Christianity. Oñate set up and governed a large colony called New Mexico.

People have lived in Cañon de Chelly for 4,000 years.

Relations between the Spanish and Indians were not always peaceful. Spanish soldiers killed Indian men. They forced Indian women and girls to work as slaves for the settlers. Sometimes the Spanish soldiers made the Pueblo fight alongside them against the Navajo. The Navajo raided Spanish settlements. Other tribes, such as the Apache, were also raiding and fighting.

Many Navajo tried to avoid the Spanish by moving to Cañon de Chelly in Arizona in the late 1700s. The area's soil was good for crops and the rocky alcoves protected them from enemies. But when the Navajo and Spanish were at war in the early 1800s, it did not offer enough protection. Spanish soldiers marched into Cañon de Chelly in 1805 and killed more than 100 women, children, and the elderly. They were hiding in a cave, which became known as **Massacre** Cave.

1805 pictograph on the canyon wall of a Spanish soldier

Mexico declared independence from Spain in 1821. Mexican settlers and soldiers invaded land that included Navajo territory. The Mexicans and Navajo became bitter enemies. Their fights continued until 1848 when Mexico lost a war with the United States. Then Americans arrived, hoping to take over the land. In response, the Navajo raided and harassed the American settlers.

massacre: the deliberate killing of a group of unarmed people

THE LONG WALK

Tensions were high between the Navajo and settlers. In the early 1860s, the U.S. government ordered the Navajo onto a **reservation**. When they refused, U.S. troops led by Colonel Christopher "Kit" Carson burned their homes and crops and contaminated their water supplies. The soldiers chopped down the Navajo's orchards and killed or drove away their animals. The Navajo had no choice but to surrender. They called the series of attacks "the fearing time."

The Navajo were forced to march more than 300 miles (483 kilometers) to the Bosque Redondo reservation. It was near Fort Sumner, in eastern New Mexico. About 8,500 Navajo survived the forced march and arrived at the fort in 1864. Some Navajo had escaped but many died along the way or were captured by slave traders. Their terrible experience became known as the Long Walk. The survivors joined about 400 Mescalero Apache who were already at Bosque Redondo. They all lived like prisoners. There was a shortage of food, drinking water, firewood, and shelters. Many more people died. The Navajo called Bosque Redondo the "place of suffering." U.S. officials finally realized the reservation was a failure. The Navajo, led by Barboncito, agreed to a **treaty** in 1868.

reservation: an area of land set aside by the government for American Indians; in Canada reservations are called reserves

treaty: an official agreement between two or more groups or countries

Many Navajo died on the Long Walk to Bosque Redondo.

The Navajo were allowed to return to their homeland. They would receive sheep, goats, cattle, and corn. The Navajo agreed to stop raids on railroad workers and settlers.

Barboncito explained how important returning home was to his people. "After we get back to our country, it will brighten up again, and the Navajos will be as happy as the land. Black clouds will lift, and there will be plenty of rain to make the corn grow. It will grow in abundance, and we shall be happy."

Navajo territory was reduced to about 5,000 square miles (13,000 square km), but land would be added in years to come. The Diné set out to rebuild their lives.

Chapter 3

Navajo Life Today

Navajo Nation Council Chamber in Window Rock, Arizona

The Navajo have adapted. But it hasn't been easy. In 1924 all American Indians became United States citizens. But the U.S. government did not always treat its new citizens well. It continued the practice of forcing Navajo and other Indian children to leave their families and live in faraway schools. They were not allowed to speak their own language. Government officials wanted American Indians to become more like white people.

In the 1930s and 1940s, another government program hurt the Navajo. They were forced to kill almost half of their sheep. Other livestock also had to be killed. The government believed this would prevent land from being overgrazed. Yet the plants and grasses that had been disappearing did not grow back as officials expected.

The first Navajo tribal government had been established in 1923 after oil was discovered on the reservation. The Navajo Tribal Council spoke for the Diné's rights and needs. It continues to serve as the government of the Navajo Nation. The council has 110 communities called chapters on the reservation. The government is based in Window Rock, Arizona. It has three branches. There is the 88-member Navajo Nation Council, the president and vice president, and a court system.

The Navajo Nation spans three states.

NAVAJO NATION

The Navajo Nation is the largest reservation in the United States. It is the second largest Indian tribe in the country by population. Only the Cherokee have more members. About 300,000 people are members of the Navajo Nation, including more than 180,000 who live on the reservation. The reservation, Diné Bikéyah, spans more than 27,000 square miles (70,000 square km) in Arizona, New Mexico, and Utah.

High flying flag
The Navajo flag was the first American Indian flag to fly into space. In 1995 astronaut Bernard Harris carried it aboard the space shuttle *Discovery*. He lived on the Navajo Nation as a child.

NAVAJO CODE TALKERS

A group of Navajo Marines played an important role in World War II (1939-1945). They sent and received secret coded messages that confused the enemy and helped the United States and its allies win the war. The code was based on the Navajo language.

In the early days of the war, wireless radios allowed U.S. troops to stay in contact with other forces. But their enemies, the Japanese, easily understood the radio messages.

The U.S. military needed a simple, unbreakable code. The solution came from a Los Angeles engineer who had grown up on the Navajo reservation. Although not Navajo himself, he knew the language. And he knew how difficult it was to learn. The code consisted of Navajo words that represented each letter in the English alphabet.

In the code, for example, the Navajo word for apple (*be-la-sana*) stood for the letter A. The 400 Navajo code talkers sent messages by using Navajo words to spell out words in English. There were also Navajo words that represented common military terms. By the end of the war the code had grown to about 600 words. The Navajo code talkers had to memorize them all. And they were fast. They could send and translate a three-line message in 20 seconds.

The Japanese never broke the code. When the war ended in 1945 and the Navajo returned home, they were told not to talk about their jobs. In 2001 President George W. Bush awarded Congressional gold medals to the 29 original code talkers. Later that year all code talkers received silver medals.

Chapter 4

Connecting to the Past

Sharing their heritage with younger generations is important to Navajo people. Many students who attend a reservation school learn the Navajo language. They study Navajo culture along with regular classes. Young people are encouraged to adopt Navajo traditions while furthering their education. After high school some students go to colleges throughout the country. Others start closer to home by attending Diné College, a two-year community college. Its main campus is in Tsaile, Arizona. It has five other community campuses on the reservation in Arizona and New Mexico.

Diné College's main building in Tsaile is shaped like a hogan.

SPORTS

Like their ancestors, some young Navajo still enjoy foot races and archery games. Basketball is the most popular sport on the reservation. School teams play against each other, drawing huge crowds. Rodeo is another popular Navajo sport. The horseback events test riders' skills, while honoring horses, which are important to Navajo history.

Basketball is a favorite sport on the reservation.

RELIGION

The Navajo are members of various churches, but most also pay tribute to versions of the Navajo original creation story. Worshipping Father Sky and Mother Earth is part of their heritage. Honoring the natural environment and remembering their ancestors are also very important.

Many Navajo people still keep a hogan for traditional ceremonies behind their modern houses. Ceremonies are associated with many aspects of everyday life. Some can last up to nine days. Most ceremonies include stories and legends about Navajo history. There is even a ceremony for a baby's first laugh.

The most religious people in Navajo culture are medicine people, also called singers. Most medicine people are men, but there are some medicine women too.

An artist depicts the creation of the four sacred mountains.

It takes singers years to learn the sacred sand paintings and ceremonial procedures. There are more than 30 Navajo ceremonies, but most medicine people specialize in only a few. The intricate sand paintings they make are always destroyed after a ceremony. It is believed that the sand absorbs negative energy.

MEDICINE

When Navajo are sick or hurt, they can see a doctor or visit a hospital on or near the Navajo Nation. The U.S. Indian Health Services Program provides medical services for American Indians. Sometimes the Navajo prefer to see traditional medicine people. Besides being the religious figures in Navajo society, they are believed to have the power to diagnose and heal illnesses. They use plants, herbs, prayers, songs, and ceremonies.

Shiprock in New Mexico looms behind a medicine man. It is a sacred place to the Navajo.

Navajo weavers in the early 1900s (right) and today

HANDCRAFTS

Many Navajo still maintain looms where they weave wool from sheep into rugs, blankets, clothing, and accessories. The wool might come from their own sheep. Weavers incorporate colorful designs that symbolize Navajo beliefs and stories. The stripes and geometric patterns sometimes indicate the region where the item was made. Navajo rugs are popular worldwide.

Like their rugs and blankets, Navajo pottery and baskets are usually made with meaningful patterns and symbols. It is believed that many of the designs were borrowed from cliff-dwelling tribes, like the Pueblo, in past centuries. The designs might include symbols for falling rain, mountains, turkey tracks, stars, whirling logs, and lightning. Many baskets are used in ceremonies.

Beautiful jewelry

Silver and turquoise jewelry made by the Navajo is in great demand around the world. The Navajo learned to work with silver during Spanish and Mexican occupations in past centuries. They originally obtained silver by melting down coins. They later added turquoise, which symbolizes water, health, and happiness.

Navajo dancers carry traditional baskets.

FOOD

Traditional Navajo recipes have been shared verbally from mother to daughter. They include ingredients that are most often measured with their hands. Goat meat and **mutton** have also been an important part of the Navajo diet for hundreds of years. Corn, beans, squash, and fry bread are popular.

A Navajo woman demonstrates the traditional way to cook fry bread.

mutton: meat from sheep that is eaten by people

CLOTHING

Men and women wear traditional Navajo styles for special occasions. Women wear velvet or cotton skirts with matching long-sleeved blouses, wide belts, and moccasins. They use yarn to tie their hair into a special bun. Men wear velvet shirts, pants, and moccasins. Silver and turquoise jewelry is a common accessory.

Number four

The number four is important to the Navajo culture. There are four sacred mountains, four seasons, four original Navajo clans, four directions, and four colors. Their artwork often reflects the number.

WORK

Navajo are employed in a wide range of occupations. Many Navajo work in the shops, offices, restaurants, and other businesses on the Navajo Nation. Ranching and raising sheep are still an important ways for many Navajo to support their families. They sell the sheep for mutton and shear the sheep for wool.

The Navajo strive to walk in harmony with the land. They do this among the colorful deserts, canyons, and mountains of their beloved Navajo Nation.

A horseman herds goats in the sand dunes of the Navajo Nation.

TIMELINE

1000–1500: Ancestors of the Navajo travel from Alaska and Canada to settle in the Southwest.

1598: Spanish leader Juan de Oñate brings settlers and herds to establish the colony of New Mexico.

1805: Spanish soldiers kill Navajo women and children in Cañon de Chelly.

1821: Mexico declares independence from Spain.

1848: The United States claims New Mexico, including Navajo territory, after the Mexican War.

1864: Thousands of Navajo are forced into the Long Walk to Bosque Redondo that kills many.

1868: Treaty between the U.S. government and the Navajo allows the Navajo to return to a reservation established on their land.

1923: Navajo Tribal Council is established.

1941–1945: About 3,600 Navajo serve in World War II.

1968: Navajo Community College is established as the first tribal-controlled community college in the United States; it changes its name to Diné College in 1997.

1969: Tribal Council establishes the reservation as the Navajo Nation.

2009: President Barack Obama signs bill that includes text apologizing to American Indians for "many instances of violence, maltreatment, and neglect."

2015: Navajo Nation imposes a 2 percent tax on junk food in an effort to curb obesity; it eliminates a 5 percent sales tax on fresh fruits and vegetables.

GLOSSARY

ancestor (AN-sess-tur)—family member who lived a long time ago

clan (KLAN)—a large group of families and related people

elder (EL-dur)—older person whose experience makes him or her a leader

massacre (MASS-uh-kuhr)—the deliberate killing of a group of unarmed people

mutton (MUHT-n)—meat from sheep that is eaten by people

reservation (rez-er-VAY-shuhn)—area of land set aside by the government for American Indians; in Canada reservations are called reserves

treaty (TREE-tee)—an official agreement between two or more groups or countries

tradition (truh-DISH-uhn)—custom, idea, or belief passed down through time

READ MORE

Collins, Terry. *Into the West: Causes and Effects of U.S. Westward Expansion.* North Mankato, Minn.: Capstone, 2014.

Birchfield, D.L., and Helen Dwyer. *Navajo History and Culture.* Native American Library. New York: Gareth Stevens Pub., 2012.

O'Dell, Scott. *Sing Down the Moon.* Boston: HMH Books for Young Readers, 2010.

INTERNET SITES

FactHound offers a safe, fun way to find Internet sites related to this book. All of the sites on FactHound have been researched by our staff.

Here's all you do:

Visit *www.facthound.com*

Type in this code: 9781491449929

Super-cool stuff! Check out projects, games and lots more at
www.capstonekids.com

CRITICAL THINKING USING THE COMMON CORE

1. In what ways do Navajo people today pay tribute to the cultural traditions of their ancestors? (Key Ideas and Details)

2. Many Navajo families today maintain a hogan, along with a modern house. How does this connect them to their past? And why is it important? (Integration of Knowledge and Ideas)

3. Despite the warring years of Spanish and Mexican occupation, the Navajo adopted influences from each culture. What were they? (Key ideas and Details)

INDEX